Camb
Contemporary
Poets
2

Edited by

Wes Magee

CAMBRIDGE
UNIVERSITY PRESS

Published by the Press Syndicate of the University of Cambridge
The Pitt Building, Trumpington Street, Cambridge CB2 1RP
40 West 20th Street, New York, NY 10011-4211, USA
10 Stamford Road, Oakleigh, Victoria, 3166, Australia

A catalogue record for this book is available from the
British Library.

Printed in Great Britain by Scotprint Ltd, Musselburgh

ISBN 0 521 39750 2 paperback

Cover and text photography by Nicholas Judd

Thanks are due to the following to reproduce photographs: p. 43
by courtesy of Andrew Nurnberg Associates; p. 53 by courtesy of
the daughter of Stanley Cook.

VN

Contents

Wes Magee

Editor's introduction

Poets of the present day come from different walks of life, and have varied backgrounds. There is no 'set' way to become a writer, a poet. Irina Ratushinskaya, for example, was incarcerated in a Russian prison for years, whereas Julie O'Callaghan grew up in Chicago, USA. Nearer home, John Cotton is a Londoner who served in the Royal Navy and experienced typhoons in the South China Sea.

The poems, also, differ greatly; there are variations in form and subject matter. Roger McGough's irrepressible Liverpudlian humour comes through in many of his poems, while Wendy Cope has a nice touch with parody. Mick Gowar's poems concentrate on adolescent experiences, acutely observed.

This book, with its eight living poets, uses poems of the present day for the reader to enjoy. Whether the poems are serious or use humour they offer interesting windows through which to view our world. And, guided by the 'Write your own poems' section, you can have a go at developing *your* creative ability.

Wes Magee

John Cotton

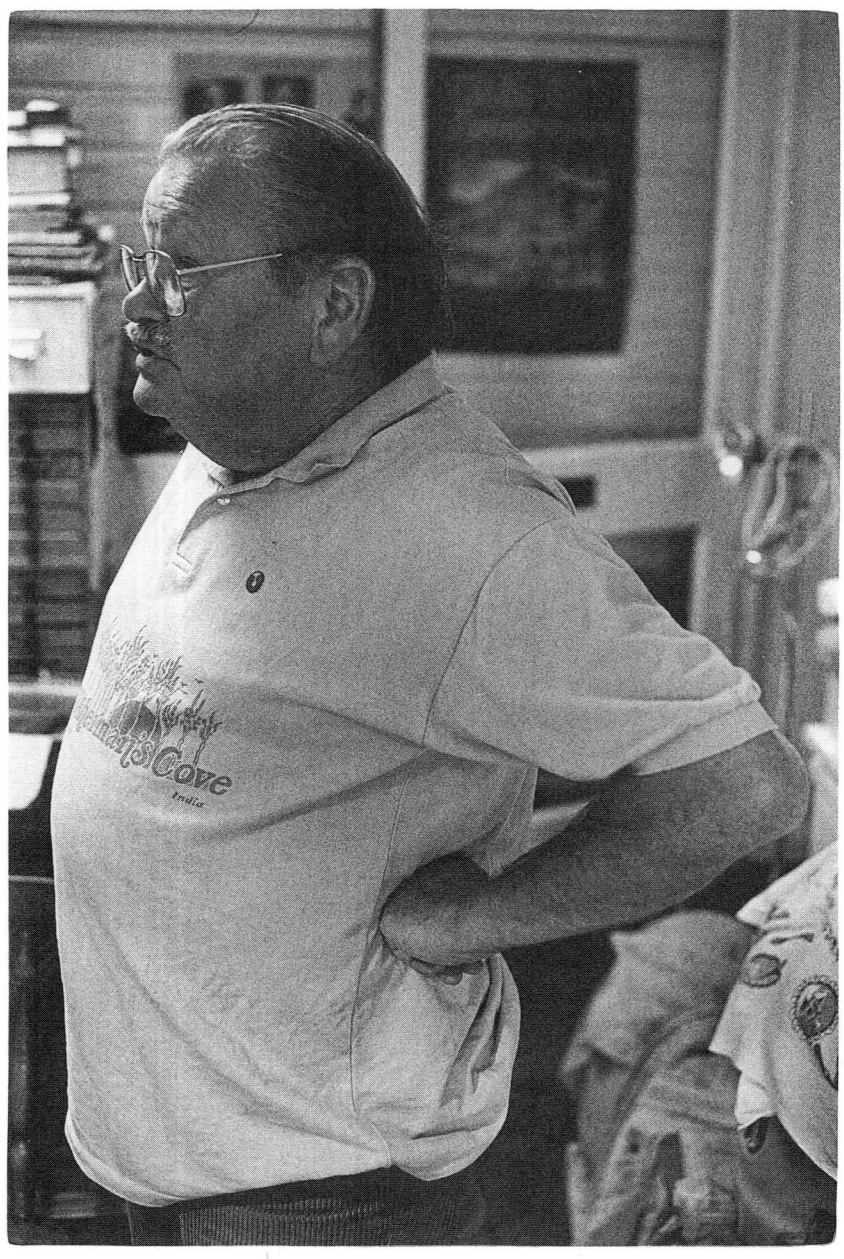

Introduction

I was born in Hackney, London. At the age of two I moved with my parents to Harrow, north London. I went to Headstone Lane, a school for all ages, the Boys' High School, Harrow, and Acton Technical College. My dad wanted me to be an engineer. I came not to enjoy school very much.

When I left school the Second World War was on, so I joined the Royal Navy as a young entrant. This, amongst other things, took me to Canada, the USA, Ceylon, India, Malaya, Sumatra, Borneo, Sarawak, the Philippines (this was accidental – we got into a typhoon in the South China Sea which blew us there!), Hong Kong, and the coast of China. So I developed a taste for travel and an interest in other peoples and their cultures.

When I left the Navy I read for a degree in English, graduated and found employment as a teacher. I had wanted to be a writer. But if you write a book you do not earn anything from it for at least two years, and then you have to be lucky! So, I had to find an immediate way of earning money.

Unfortunately for me I was quite good at teaching, gained promotion and was stuck. I taught mainly in Wealdstone, Southall and Hemel Hempstead where I was a headteacher.

I did write of course, novels. I wrote three novels which took about eighteen months to two years each, and I got nowhere. I wanted to write poetry, but I thought poets were a special kind of people and I was not all that special. Then I found myself working in Southall with a poet, a good one named Ted Walker. Poets weren't special in the way I had thought. What is special about a poet is the poetry he or she writes. So, I began writing poetry, though rather late in life. After a few years I had some success and my first book of poems *Old Movies*, was published by Chatto and Windus. Poets have to keep grafting and not be discouraged. The other thing is that, like teaching, writing is a job for those who believe in it.

So what do you have to believe? It is the same for both teaching and writing. You have to believe it is important that people are helped to understand themselves and the world in which they live. You have to believe in Democracy where such understanding is essential if people are to use their vote wisely. That is why some politicians are not very keen on education or poetry!

In my writing I try to explore my thoughts, beliefs, feelings and experiences, and the words and language I use. Fun is important of course as, while you have to take the art seriously, you must not take yourself so.

For the past five years I have been a freelance writer. That is, I find work where I can. Sometimes I spend time in schools talking to teachers and boys and girls about writing and poetry. That is when I began writing for young people. Sometimes I will spend time in a school being known as the 'writer in residence'. In such employment I have worked in schools in Bishop's Stortford, Felsted, Peterborough and I completed a tour of schools in Germany.

I like eating, drinking, conversation, walking, music – classical and jazz, travelling, reading, theatre and films. I get about a bit. Otherwise being stuck on your own, writing in a study, can be a bit antisocial. Besides, you have to experience things in order to write.

I have two sons, and three grandchildren, Tamsin, Barnaby and Phoebe.

Birthplace	Hackney, London
School	Boys' High School, Harrow
Further Education	Acton Technical College
Favourite sport	Support Tottenham Hotspur
Musical interest	Classical (Bach, Chopin), jazz (Bix Biederbecke, Fats Waller)
Favourite food	Hot lime pickle sandwich with a side plate of chillis
Favourite drink	Pint of Murphy's stout
Best TV programme	''Allo 'Allo'
Best radio programme	'I'm sorry, I haven't a clue'
Travels abroad	Europe (France, Germany, Spain, Italy, Greece), USA and Canada, Israel, China and the Far East, Eastern Europe (Hungary, Romania, Turkey)
Favourite books (as a child)	*Treasure Island* by R. L. Stevenson, *The Jungle Book* by Rudyard Kipling
Favourite poets	Lots ... including William Cowper, Matthew Arnold, Carol Ann Duffy, Kit Wright, Alan Brownjohn and Jason Strugnell
Comment on 'green' issues	Support conservation
Hobbies	Printing (I run a small press at home), beer-making, collecting model pigs, wearing odd socks, listening to the silence
Ambition	To own a spinach farm
Pets	A Jack Russell dog called 'Oscar'
Preferred transport	Trains, slow boats, the top of a double-decker bus

11

Listen

Silence is when you can hear things.
Listen:
The breathing of bees,
A moth's footfall,
Or the mist easing its way
Across the field,
The light shifting at dawn
Or the stars clicking into place
At evening.

In the kitchen

In the kitchen
After the aimless
Chatter of the plates,
The murmuring of the gas,
The chuckles of the water pipes
And the sharp exchanges
Of the knives, forks and spoons,
Comes the serious quiet
When the sink slowly clears its throat,
And you can hear the occasional rumble
Of the refrigerator's tummy
As it digests the cold.

Totleigh riddles

1   Silent I invade cities,
    Blur edges, confuse travellers,
    My thumb smudging the light.
    I drift from rivers
    To loiter in early morning fields,
    Until Constable Sun
    Moves me on.

2   I work while you sleep,
    Needing no light to etch windows
    Or elaborate leaf or branch.
    Without colour my wonder is
    My patterns within patterns
    Growing like crisp stars.
    Look, but do not touch.
    Your warmth is my end.

3   We are a crystal zoo,
    Wielders of fortunes,
    The top of our professions.
    Like hard silver nails
    Hammered into the dark
    We make charts for mariners.

4   I reveal your secrets.
    I am your morning enemy,
    Though I give reassurance of presence.
    I can be magic,
    Or the judge in beauty contests.
    Count Dracula has no use for me.
    When you leave
    I am left to my own reflections.

5 Rain polishes
   My round the year gloss,
   Honing my row
   Of sharp spears.
   In winter I come into my own,
   Bearing the crown
   And gifts
   Of bright beads of blood.

6 A great cold cinder,
   At year's end I face the sun
   Across pale watered skies,
   Outshone but not outpulled.
   Ruling tides, blood and calendars,
   I float on water, bend minds,
   And like knowledge
   Illumine but not warm.

6 Moon.
1 Fog or mist; 2 Frost; 3 Stars; 4 Mirror; 5 Holly;
Answers

Only

Only a tap drip, dripping
In the courtyard by the wall,
Where cushiony mosses flourish
And fleshy ferns grow tall.
Only a shutter rattling
When the wind decides to call.
Only a creeping of shadows
As night begins to fall.
Only a whisper of memories
In the lonely air of the hall.

The Wilderness

'This is the wilderness,' my uncle said:
A corner of the garden he'd let go,
Grass waist high and trees grown spindly
Because they were too close together,
A contrast to the rose beds, well mown lawn
And ranks of vegetables. There we would play
Where Indians, outlaws and rugged pioneers
Haunted the patch of wonder surviving
In a suburb. It's all gone now: childhood, uncle,
The patch sold to more determined gardeners.
To remember is to miss that place
Where imagination grew, lost now
In the cautious cultivation of our days.
'All gardens should have one,' uncle said.
We should have listened to him.

They hide to watch me

They hide to watch me as I walk the woods.
The squirrels from their gables in the trees,
While the foxglove's thimbles shade the questing bees.
On the trunks of beeches moths merge with the bark
And soft-eyed deer stare cautious from the dark
Of thickets where blackbirds lurk and peer,
To dart in further should I draw too near.
The woodpecker pauses from her busy drumming
To warn the others that a stranger's coming.
A quick white flash, the rabbit's dived for cover,
So have his brothers, sisters, cousins, aunts – and mother!
Then all is quiet and still as nature broods
As they hide to watch me as I walk the woods.

Moorland signals

Behind the stone cottage
the wife pegs out her washing,
a bright bunting
of challenge to the grey
power of the moor
which, like the vasts
of a terrestrial sea, casts
up, from time to time,
a pony or a sheep.
Out of the mists and rime
such visitors stare at night
at the homing beacon
of the cottage's square of light.

Julie O'Callaghan

Introduction

When I was little, I promised myself one thing – that I would never grow up. I was perfectly happy with the way things were. I didn't want anything to change. I can remember watching stupid, loud teenagers and turning away in disgust, hoping the big miracle would come and I could always stay young. When other girls in my class were longing for lipstick and discos, I was at home longing to escape time.

It is the curse of a happy childhood – nothing afterwards lives up to the excitement you felt back then. Our house on Pratt Boulevard in Chicago must have resembled the house in 'There was an old woman who lived in a shoe, she had so many children, she didn't know what to do'. It was usually packed with friends, cousins, classmates and neighbours. Each of the seven children in our family had a personal contingent rattling through the house on four levels, forming clubs, repairing bicycles, playing hide and seek, baking brownies or painting and colouring at the big dining room table. A woman, passing our house one day, looked over the white picket fence and asked me if this was an orphanage.

The best part of being a child, I thought, was how you never knew what would happen next. On a cold, windy November evening after school we were told to put warm coats on and we drove down to the beach for a cook-out over a campfire. My parents planned trips and outings and parties as fast as they could think of them. Something crazy was always about to happen. When you grew up, you had to go to work and get money and pay bills and all your brothers and sisters would live in different places and it would be terrible – I could tell that much already.

It was like paradise to sit in the back seat of the car on a warm night with your chin sticking out of the rolled-down window as rows of yellow sky-scraper lights flashed by. I whispered to myself, *I'll never forget this night*; and it was true.

Nobody in my family is interested in poetry. There weren't any poetry books decorating our coffee table. The books we read were covered in plastic from the Rogers Park Public Library. Some of the pages would be stuck together with peanut butter and jelly or chocolate dribbles. We learned more at school about diving into swimming pools and Rules of the Road than about poetry. The first poem I wrote was for homework. It was written in the shape of a tree. I did other poems in the shape of my hand, the sun and a cockroach. They weren't poems I put much feeling into, I was just enjoying myself. It was only after I came to Ireland when I was twenty that I started writing more often. I'm sure it had something to do with homesickness. I wanted to use American speech and slang in my poems so that they would sound like people I knew in Chicago.

Now that I have some books published, I can't understand how it all happened. I read to schools frequently and I love to see how Irish kids react to poems with an American setting. Television seems to have helped me in that respect. Even children in small country schools now know the rules of American football and how to ride a skateboard and obscure slang. I don't need to explain what McDonald's is anymore.

I still think I had a better deal when I was young – but I can now revive those days through words:

> between sandwiches and tacos
> the drama unfolds
> some guy gets a bullet someplace
> we find where the cookies were hidden
> through the dark we hear bare feet
> shuffling on bare floorboards
> and hide the cookies
> *why aren't you kids in bed*

There *are* compensations for being grown-up – at least you can eat cookies whenever you want.

* from *Edible Anecdotes* (number 22) by Julie O'Callaghan (Dolmen Press)

Birthplace	Chicago, Illinois, USA
Brothers/sisters	Three brothers, three sisters
School	St Ignatius Grammar School, Sullivan High School
Further Education	Two years at Antioch College
Favourite sport	Showjumping and I enjoy fly-swatting
Musical interest	Classical — my favourite composers are Mahler and Bach
Favourite food	Chocolate meringue pie
Favourite drink	Cocoa with floating marshmallows
Best TV programme	'Ruby Wax in Russia'
Best radio programme	'Poet of the month'
Travels abroad	Norway, France, Austria, Germany, Canada and England. Since I live in a foreign place I'm always 'abroad', I think!
Favourite book (as a child)	*Misty* by Marguerite Henry (it's about Chincoteague Island off Maryland where wild ponies live)
Favourite poets	Robert Frost, Philip Larkin, W. S. Graham, Frank O'Hara, Robert Hass, James Schuyler, John Berryman, Marina Tsvetayeva
Comment on 'green' issues	I try to re-cycle and to buy things without too much packaging, and I use lead-free petrol
Hobbies	Knitting difficult patterns
Ambition	To win a million pounds (punts) in the Irish Lotto. I would buy a house in America and a farm in Ireland
Pets	If I had a pet it would be a dove-grey Great Dane which I would name Cornelius
Preferred transport	Horse

The beach trail

That was the most tedious journey
ever travelled, the most torturous trail
known to mankind:
at five thirty on a summer evening
with our gritty teeth,
our smelly towels,
with our buckets of rare stones
and shoes full of shells never before seen,
with our ears full of sand,
our skin burning,
our hair decorated with seaweed,
with a piece of glass in our heel,
our mother's radio,
our cousin's beachball,
with an ice cream bar in our stomachs,
a special hunk of driftwood,
an arm, neck and leg full of mosquito bites,
our bathing suits damp and itchy,
with our tempers frayed,
our gym shoes lost,
our money spent,
our holes dug,
our castles wrecked,
our sand battles won,
we paraded down the street
and back to civilization
as we knew it.

Happy birthday from Bennigans

Why did you do it, Mother?
I told you – didn't I – that I'd go with you
to a restaurant for my birthday
on one condition: Don't go and blab
to the waitress it's my BIG DAY.
But you had to go and tell her.
God, what if somebody had seen me?
I realise that you and Daddy
simply do not care if you ruin my reputation.
I almost thought for a teensy second
you had restrained yourself for once.
But no. You and your big mouth.
'Hip, hop, happy, b, birth, day,
hap, hap, happy, Happy Birthday to You!':
a zero girl, singing a zero song
at the top of her nothingness of a voice.
'All of us at Bennigans hope it's a special day!'
All of them, Mother, not just some.
That's IT for birthdays from now on.
Next year I'll be celebrating by myself.

Touring company

In the gymnasium children dressed as mice
practised their steps to the beat of a cane.
The floor was planted with bright tutus
waiting for ballerinas to claim them.
The orchestra repeated a difficult passage.
In the wings of the stage,
dancers were bending and stretching.
The dressing room was crowded
with yanking and tugging girls
spraying perfume, holding their breath
while someone zipped them up.
They pushed their faces close to mirrors
applying cartoon eyebrows and cheeks.
The wardrobe mistress smiled a mouthful of pins
while she tucked up a hem on her hands and knees.
A princess clipped her crown in place,
picked up a powder puff
and created a dust storm around her shoulders.
A green-faced witch bent down
and asked me if I wanted to be a dancer.
I nodded with goosebumps
travelling along my spine.

Swan Lake

Tonight, when all the other girls rush
to the station or bus stop to get home fast
for a TV dinner and television,
I won't be in a hurry.

I'll casually cross the street to McDonald's
and while eating I'll imagine
what it's like after the overture
as the curtain goes up on Swan Lake.

I bought the second-most expensive ticket
on my lunch-break. I don't know how
I can wait two-and-a-half more hours until I get out.
It was just a whim – I was bored with the same old routine.

The girls thought I had a big date when they saw me.
I told them I was going to the ballet.
The palaces, princes and magic forest
will be waiting for me to finish my hamburger.

FROM Edible Anecdotes (*number 9*)

Jimmy Dean stood outside a model Western saloon
signing autographs with diamond cuff links glittering
and pointy cowboy boots wishing they could run away
as we entered the Wisconsin State Fair
it was an iridescent midwestern day
so we rode the ferris wheel
screaming as we flew over the top
catching the breeze in our ears
I won a set of china ponies with feather manes
and we all sat down to free brochures
on pig feed and tractors
licking fudgicles and cotton candy

FROM Edible Anecdotes (*number 22*)

the film about some war
has just begun with a lion yawning
it is midnight
you make the refrigerator copy the lion
and our eyes starved for light
move across the shelves
hunting for the thing
our stomachs have always wanted
but never found
the light bulb on the side
shines through the wire shelves
and makes the ceiling our cage
between sandwiches and tacos
the drama unfolds
some guy gets a bullet someplace
we find where the cookies were hidden
through the dark we hear bare feet
shuffling on bare floorboards
and hide the cookies
why aren't you kids in bed

Local man tells of native city

Well, it's my kinda town, for one.
Ya got yer Cubs, White Sox, Bears and Black Hawks
and as for that faggoty game they play
over there in Europe
– kick the ball – well I tell ya,
we got that one too
only I ain't gonna brag about it, see?
As for yer public recreation and leisure areas,
there's Lincoln Park which includes the Farm in the Zoo,
for the city kids to see cows and pigs
and it's always a big hit, stuff like that,
with my kids, anyway. Some a the company
in them places ain't too choice
as every pervert and louse seems to be
hanging around the park lately,
but for a Sunday outing yer safe enough.
Anywho, in a place like this, ya can't
exactly keep yer offspring in the dark
about weirdos and life in general
if ya know what I mean
with guys doin' indecent things on the subway, etc.
Chicago's Finest ain't got the easiest job
in the whole wide world, and I always
make it easier for them wonderful guys
by keeping a ten dollar bill in my pocket,
not to mention my twelve-year-old, Judy,
who's a genius at turning on
the waterworks in an emergency.
Then we come to State Street, that great street
where they do things they don't do on Broadway.
If ya want my advice you'll stick
to the east side a that place because
for I-don't-know-how-long the west side
is kinda seamy or somethin, don't ask me why.
If yer hungry go eat a sandwich or a piece of cake
in this joint called The Palmer House
and you'll feel pretty ritzy in the cafeteria.
Wabash Avenue is my idea of a real man's street

with a capital M. It's dark, cuz
the elevated tracks run overhead and it's got
stuff like camera shops, steak restaurants,
and if you're driving down that street,
it's a challenge avoiding the steel girders
that hold up the tracks; Abe Lincoln
would a liked Wabash Avenue I think.
My wife tells me that all the classy types
have moved up to North Michigan Avenue,
but from what I've seen it looks like
a crowd of conventioneers from hicky places
like Cairo, Illinois and Dubuque, Iowa,
with badges saying 'Hi, I'm Selma' on them.
The Playboy Club is up there, I admit,
but if my wife says the classy types
hang around there, well ya can bet yer bottom dollar
that they've cleared out and left it
for the Japs, suburbanites and hicks.
If you're really bored it's nice to go out to
O'Hare Airport and watch everybody
leaving and coming or check the phones
for change – I once collected eight dollars.
Each time I roam Chicago keeps calling me home.
It's one town that won't let you down.

A sunny day

The sun is shining
here in Ireland
so I decide to phone my mother
in America far away.
'Hi!' I say to her, 'it's me –
take out your sunglasses.'
She puts down the telephone
and gets a pair of shades.
'Are you there again?' I ask her.
'Now look outside at the sun: warm, right?'
She says, 'Yes, it's warm here,
the sun is beating down into this room.'
'Hey!' I say, 'it's on my hand
and on my knee, the same sunny day!'

Roger McGough

Roger McGough talks to himself

(The writer talked to the performer in the dressing-room after a poetry reading.)

Did you enjoy this evening?
    Yes, I think it went quite well.

Do you do a lot of these events?
    Not really. If I perform too often then there isn't time for writing. It's a question of balance. I enjoy performing because I get to travel around the world, and the pay is good, but my main interest is with the written word. I am happiest when I am writing.

So, when you're not on stage, you are writing?
    Unfortunately, no. I spend a lot of time messing about. Doodling and making excuses.

Were you interested in poetry at school?
    Not really. My mother sent me to elocution classes when I was about 12, because I spoke too fast (still do), and ranallthewordstogether. I enjoyed reciting poetry and doing choral verse, but I never wrote anything. The language of the poems I was made to study seemed old-fashioned (and I wasn't).

When did you begin writing then?
    At Hull University. I always had a secret ambition to be a painter, and being an impressionable youth loved the Impressionists. While studying French I began reading the poets who were writing at the time of Van Gogh, Cézanne and the rest, and copied the poems instead of the painting.

Finally, I am sure some of our younger readers would be interested in hearing about your days in Liverpool as a member of the 'Scaffold'. Recording with the likes of Jimi Hendrix, Paul McCartney, Elton John. Would you like to talk about that?
    No.

Oh ... er ... thanks, anyway.
    It's been a pleasure.

34

Birthplace	Liverpool
Brothers/sisters	One sister, a nurse
School	'Star of the Sea' Junior School, St Mary's College
Further education	Hull University
Favourite sport	Cricket, snooker, table-tennis, football (support Everton)
Favourite food	Fried parsnips
Best TV programme	Live football
Best radio programme	'Pick of the week'
Travels abroad	Australia, Hong Kong, Czechoslovakia, and most of Europe
Favourite book (as a child)	*Treasure Island* by R. L. Stevenson
Favourite poets	Charles Causley, Kit Wright, Brian Patten, James Reeves, Adrian Mitchell, Adrian Henri, Norman MacCaig
Comment on 'green' issues	Can't drive, and don't wish to
Hobbies	Collecting inkwells
Preferred transport	Uncrowded trains

The man who steals dreams

Santa Claus has a brother
A fact few people know
He does not have a friendly face
Nor a beard as white as snow

He does not climb down chimneys
Nor ride in an open sleigh
He is not kind and giving
But cruelly takes away

He is not fond of children
Or grown-ups who are kind
And emptiness the only gift
That he will leave behind

He is wraith, he is silent
He is greyness of steam
And if you're sleeping well tonight
Then hang on to your dream

He is sour, he is stooping
His cynic's cloak is black
And if he takes your dream away
You never get it back

Dreams with happy endings
With ambition and joy
Are the ones that he seeks
To capture and destroy

So, if you don't believe in Santa
Or in anything at all
The chances are his brother
Has already paid a call.

Green piece

Show me a salad
  and I'll show you a sneeze
Anything green
  makes me weak at the knees
On St Patrick's Day
  I stay home and wheeze
I have hay fever all the year round.

Broken-down lawnmowers
  Bring me out in a sweat
A still-life of flowers,
  in oils, and I get
All the sodden signs
  of a sinus upset
I have hay fever all the year round.

A chorus of birdsong
  makes my flesh creep
I dream of a picnic
  and scratch in my sleep
Counting pollen
  instead of sheep
I have hay fever all the year round.

Summertime's great
  (except for the sun)
Holly and mistletoe
  make my nose run
Autumn leaves and I swoon
  it's no fun
Having hay fever all the year round.

Laughing, all the way to Bank

The beautiful girl
in the flowing white dress
struggled along the platform
at the Angel.

In one hand
she carried a large suitcase.
In the other, another.

On reaching me
she stopped. Green eyes flashing
like stolen butterflies.

'Would you be so kind
as to carry one for me,'
she asked, 'as far as Bank?'

I laughed. 'My pleasure.'
And it was. Safe from harm,
All the way to Bank,
Moist in my palm, one green eye.

The end of summer

It is the end of summer
The end of day and cool,
As children, holiday-sated,
Idle happily home from school.
Dusk is slow to gather
The pavements still are bright,
It is the end of summer
And a bag of dynamite

Is pushed behind the counter
Of a department store, and soon
A trembling hand will put an end
To an English afternoon.
The sun on rooftops gleaming
Underlines the need to kill,
It is the end of summer
And all is cool, and still.

Three rusty nails

Mother, there's a strange man
Waiting at the door
With a familiar sort of face
You feel you've seen before.

Says his name is Jesus
Can we spare a couple of bob
Says he's been made redundant
And now can't find a job.

Yes I think he is a foreigner
Egyptian or a Jew
Oh aye, and that reminds me
He'd like some water too.

Well shall I give him what he wants
Or send him on his way?
OK I'll give him 5p
Say that's all we've got today.

And I'll forget about the water
I suppose it's a bit unfair
But honest, he's filthy dirty
All beard and straggly hair.

*   *   *   *   *

Mother, he asked about the water
I said the tank had burst
Anyway I gave him the coppers
That seemed to quench his thirst.

He said it was little things like that
That kept him on the rails
Then he gave me his autographed picture
And these three rusty nails.

Estate

Mother!
They're building a towncentre in the bedroom
A carpark in the lounge, it's a sin.

There's a block of flats going up in the toilet
What a shocking estate we are in.

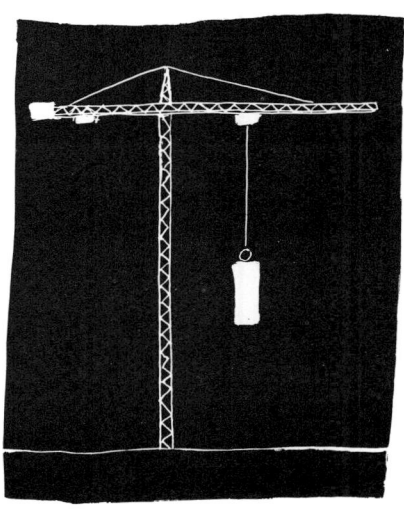

Cardiff 6pm

No. 12 a long room built under the eaves.
Tri-angular. Like living in a giant Toblerone packet.
One-bar electric fire and a meter only takes
threepenny bits. Sore throat and a cold a comin
sure as eggs is eggs is eggs.
Somewhere between here and London
the van has broken down. No band.
No props. It's going to be a fun show
at the Barry Memorial Hall.
'Drink Brains' says the advert on a beermat.
They'd drink anything down here.
Must be the coaldust and all that
choirpractice. Outside it's raining oldwomen
and walkingsticks. The pillow feels damp.
Tears of the previous paying guest.
The eskimos in the room next door
speak fluent welsh at the tops
of their voices. Not a drink to be had
TB or not TB that is the question.
Pneumonia at least. Sure as eggs
is eggs is eggs is eggs is eggs
is eggs is eggs is eggs is eggs
is eggs croeso is eggs is eggs is eggs
is eggs is eggs is eggs is eggs
is eggs is eggs is eggs is eggs

Irina Ratushinskaya

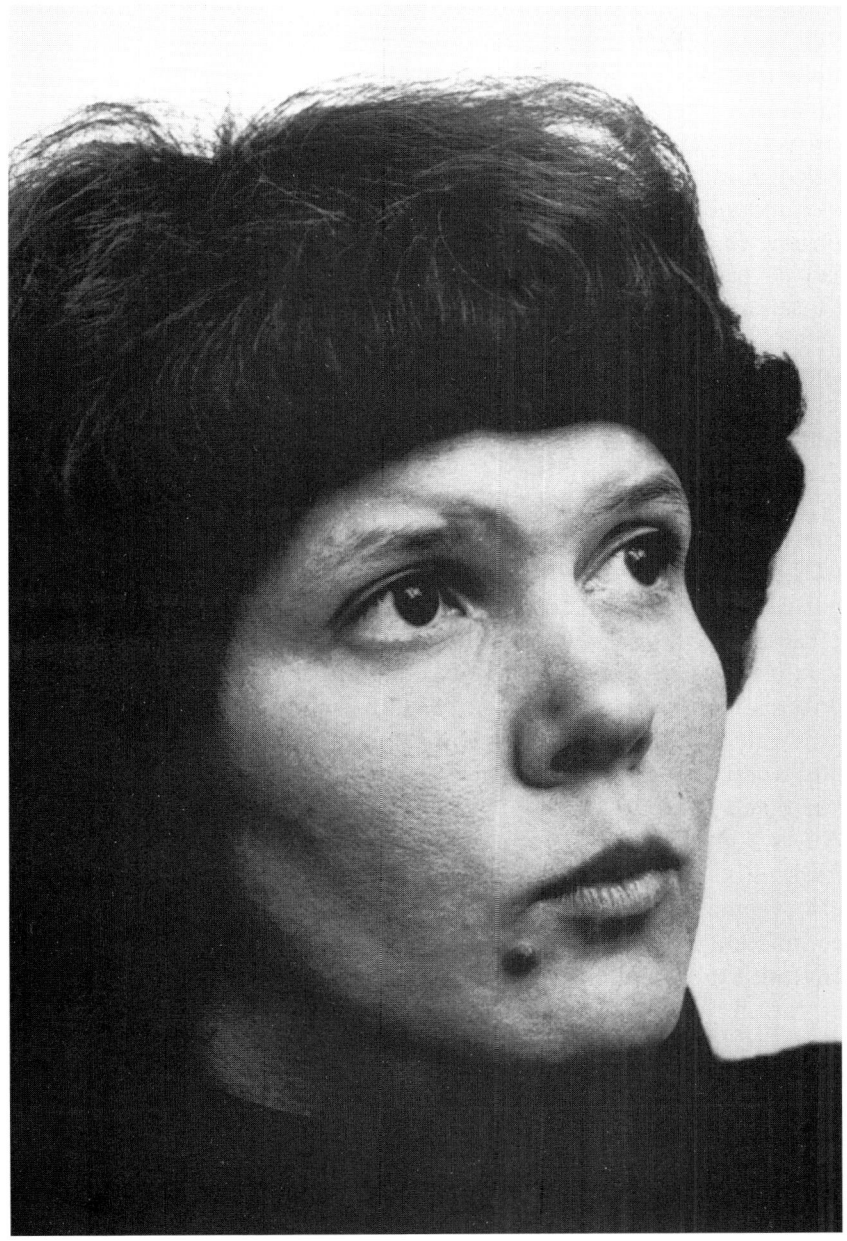

Introduction

Irina Georgievna Ratushinskaya was born in Odessa, Ukrainian SSR, on 4 March 1954. Her parents, the descendants of Russified Polish ex-gentry, who had managed to adapt to conditions of life in Russia after the Soviet takeover, brought her up in a conventional fashion, according to the strictures of Soviet cultural and political orthodoxy. Her school education was also of a model Soviet kind, and she rebelled against it early on, unable to adopt the postulates and required attitudes of the Soviet 'religion'. Instead, she acquired a faith in Catholic Christianity, the religion of her grandparents. A lively-spirited child, she soon came into conflict with the Soviet authorities; the conflicts continued into her adolescence and adulthood.

Although she had loved literature from an early age, Ratushinskaya chose not to specialise in these as subjects of formal study, since in the Soviet Union most discussion of the humanities is permeated by ideological concepts and is a thoroughly risky enterprise, exposing those who participate in it to the danger of expressing political heresies which are punishable by law. Instead, she opted to study natural science. In 1976 she received a diploma degree in physics, and accepted a teaching position at the Odessa Pedagogical Institute. While at university, she had experimented with writing, mostly of a light, dramatic kind, producing scripts for humorous student revues, and a few poems. She did not begin to write in earnest until, during the late 1970s, she discovered the poetry of the Russian 'Silver Age', and that of the great 'quartet' of Russian poets: Akhmatova, Mandelstam, Pasternak and Tsvetayeva. The discovery of these poets (whom she read in the hard-to-obtain complete and semi-complete Western and Soviet editions circulating unofficially among the students) was an intense and profound spiritual experience for her, and after it she began to write her own poems with a greatly increased seriousness and sense of artistic commitment.

In 1979 she married the human rights activist Igor Gerashchenko, moved with him to Kiev, and became involved in the human rights movement after they were several times refused permission to emigrate. Ratushinskaya and Gerashchenko were interrogated on several occasions by the KGB and in

44

August 1981 were threatened with criminal prosecution. On 10 December 1981 they were both arrested in Moscow's Pushkin Square, where they had gone to take part in the traditional annual demonstration by dissidents (on this occasion it was in support of Andrei Sakharov) and were sentenced to 10 days' imprisonment, which Ratushinskaya served in Butyrki Prison.

On 17 September 1982 Ratushinskaya was arrested again. At her trial six months later the main charge against her was 'agitation carried on for the purpose of subverting or weakening the Soviet regime'. Cited in evidence was the fact that she had written and circulated poems critical of the Soviet Union.

One day after her 29th birthday, on 5 March 1983, Ratushinskaya was sentenced to seven years' hard labour (to be served in a 'strict regime' concentration camp), to be followed by five years of internal exile. The trial had lasted three days. The court had appointed the lawyer for Ratushinskaya's defence. She had not been permitted to conduct her own defence; she had not been allowed to complete her final testimony.

She was deported to the 'strict regime' camp at Barashevo, three hundred miles south-east of Moscow. In the harsh conditions of the camp, Ratushinskaya was treated severely for being involved in many protest strikes, along with a dozen other women political prisoners. In August 1983 she went on a three-day hunger strike after being refused a visit from her husband. The visit was granted, but other hunger strikes followed.

Between December 1983 and February 1984 she spent a total of 39 days in an unheated punishment cell (SHIZO), where she contracted pneumonia. The mortality rate in the camp was high. One report states that in 1976, 135 prisoners died there, 34 of them by suicide. 17 of these were women. 12 prisoners died in the same type of punishment cell as the one in which Ratushinskaya was held.

Irina Ratushinskaya was freed on 9th October 1986. She was allowed to leave the Soviet Union, with her husband, to come to Britain.

The sparrows of Butyrki

Now even the snow has grown sad –
Let your overwhelmed reason go,
And let's smoke our cigarettes through the air-vent,
Let's at least set the smoke free.
A sparrow flies up –
And looks at us with a searching eye:
'Share your crust with me!'
And in honourable fashion you share it with him.
The sparrows know
Whom to ask for bread.
Even though there's a double grille on the windows –
And only a crumb can get through.
What do they care
Whether you're on trial or not?
If you've fed them, you're OK.
The real trial lies ahead.
You can't entice a sparrow –
Kindness and talents are no use.
He won't tap
At the city double-glazing.
In order to understand birds
You have to be a convict.
And if you share your bread –
It means your time is done.

(11–20 December 1981)

46

But we shall remain

But we shall remain
On the squares of the monstrous chessboard –
We are all convicts.
Our coffee
Smells of burnt letters,
And a smell of opened mail fills
The post offices.
The high-rise blocks have gone deaf –
And there's no one there to shout 'Don't!'
And the stucco faces on the house fronts
Have closed their eyes.
And every night
The birds fly out of the town,
And blindly
Our dawns are lit.
Wait!
Perhaps this is only a dream.
But in the morning
The newspapers appear.

Steeply the stars are scattered

Steeply the stars are scattered, and cold in the settlements of the
    heavens.
This moon is on the wing – hold on, don't let your grip slacken!
It closes your eyes – and beyond the limits of tired vision
A skater, like a pair of compasses, draws measured circles.
In winter's black-and-white engraving nuances disappear,
The stern poverty of phrases rumbles like an oration.
Five paces to the window and four from wall to wall,
And the mounted eye blinks through the iron.
The monotonous guile of an interrogation trails past,
The young escort is guilelessly coarse in soldierly fashion ...
Oh, what calmness – to wander silently through the winter,
Not even allowing the word 'no' to fall from cracked, sewn-up
    lips!
The snowy pendulum has worn away: how many weeks have
    passed?
Only the eye is darker above the poem, the forehead hotter.
Through heat and cold – I will reach, I will reach April!
I am already on the road. And God's hand is on my shoulder.

(October 1982)

I will live and survive

I will live and survive and be asked:
How they slammed my head against a trestle,
How I had to freeze at nights,
How my hair started to turn grey...
But I'll smile. And will crack some joke
And brush away the encroaching shadow.
And I will render homage to the dry September
That became my second birth.
And I'll be asked: 'Doesn't it hurt you to remember?'
Not being deceived by my outward flippancy.
But the former names will detonate in my memory –
Magnificent as old cannon.
And I will tell of the best people in all the earth,
The most tender, but also the most invincible,
How they said farewell, how they went to be tortured,
How they waited for letters from their loved ones.
And I'll be asked: what helped us to live
When there were neither letters nor any news – only walls,
And the cold of the cell, and the blather of official lies,
And the sickening promises made in exchange for betrayal.
And I will tell of the first beauty
I saw in captivity.
A frost-covered window! No spyholes, nor walls,
Nor cell-bars, nor the long-endured pain –
Only a blue radiance on a tiny pane of glass,
A cast pattern – none more beautiful could be dreamt!
The more clearly you looked, the more powerfully blossomed
Those brigand forests, campfires and birds!
And how many times there was bitter cold weather
And how many windows sparkled after that one –
But never was it repeated,
That upheaval of rainbow ice!
And anyway, what good would it be to me now,
And what would be the pretext for that festival?
Such a gift can only be received once,
And perhaps is only needed once.

(30 November 1983)

49

To my unknown friend

Above my half of the world
The comets spread their tails.
In my half of the century
Half the world looks me in the eye.
In my hemisphere the wind's blowing,
There are feasts of plague without end.
But a searchlight shines in our faces,
And effaces the touch of death.
And our madness retreats from us,
And our sadnesses pass through us,
And we stand in the midst of our fates,
Setting our shoulders against the plague.
We shall hold it back with our selves,
We shall stride through the nightmare.
It will not get further than us – don't be afraid
On the other side of the globe!

(26 February 1984)

I sit on the floor

I sit on the floor, leaning against the radiator –
A southerner, no-gooder!
Long shadows stretch from the grating, following the lamp.
It's very cold.
You want to roll yourself into a ball, chicken-style.
Silently I listen to the night,
Tucking my chin between my knees.
A quiet rumble along the pipe:
Maybe they'll send hot water in!
But it's doubtful.
The climate's SHIZO. Cainozoic era.
What will warm us quicker – a firm ode of Derzhavin,
A disfavoured greeting of Martial,
Or Homer's bronze?
Mashka Mouse has filched a rusk
And is nibbling it behind the latrine pail.
A two-inch robber,
The most innocent thief in the world.
Outside the window there's a bustle –
And into our cell bursts –
Fresh from freedom –
The December brigand wind.
The pride of the Helsinki group doesn't sleep –
I can hear them by their breathing.
In the Perm camp the regime's
Infringer doesn't sleep either.
Somewhere in Kiev another, obsessed,
Is twiddling the knob of the radio...
And Orion ascends,
Passing from roof to roof.
And the sad tale of Russia
(Maybe we are only dreaming?)
Makes room for Mashka Mouse, and us and the radio set,
On the clean page, not yet begun,
Opening this long winter
On tomorrow.

No, I'm not afraid

No, I'm not afraid: after a year
Of breathing these prison nights
I will survive into the sadness
To name which is escape.

The cockerel will weep freedom for me
And here – knee-deep in mire –
My gardens shed their water
And the northern air blows in draughts.

And how am I to carry to an alien planet
What are almost tears, as though towards home . . .
It isn't true, I *am* afraid, my darling!
But make it look as though you haven't noticed.

Stanley Cook

Introduction

I was born and brought up in Austerfield, a small south Yorkshire village where everyone knew everyone else. It was an out-of-the-way place where people were free to indulge their little (and large) oddities. Centuries before, a local man, William Bradford, had gone from Austerfield to sail in the 'Mayflower' as a leader of the Pilgrim Fathers, and there were still equally independent characters in Austerfield in my day. People are the most fascinating subject for poetry.

I went to a two-room village school with an age range from five to fourteen. It had an enterprising headteacher who I remember read Matthew Arnold's 'Baldur Dead' to us. At eleven I went to Doncaster Grammar school, walking through fields to catch the train, pulled by 'Mallard' or some LNER engine, to town. I read a lot of books and did lots of homework on that train. Later I went to Christ Church college, Oxford University, where I read English and attended the lectures of Tolkien and C. S. Lewis. I went into teaching, working in schools in Lancashire and Yorkshire, and then lectured at Huddersfield Polytechnic.

I can remember my parents being pleasantly surprised by something I had written when I was quite young. It was before the days of 'creative writing', but at Doncaster Grammar school I did a great deal of formal writing – compositions, essays, and Latin and French proses. At Oxford I wrote poetry for my own and my friends' amusement.

When I took up teaching I wrote articles on teaching English for magazines and on south Yorkshire people and places for *The Guardian*. Gradually I began to concentrate on poetry as the most economical use of the imagination, where fourteen lines of a sonnet can bring you to the point of feeling that takes a novelist 70,000 words. I had poems published in magazines and won the Cheltenham Festival Poetry Competition in 1972. At a poetry reading in Manchester I met Harry Chambers of Peterloo Poets who offered to publish a collection of my poems and altogether published four: 'Signs of Life', 'Form Photograph', 'Staff Photograph' and 'Alphabet'. When he felt unable to publish my long poem, 'Woods beyond a cornfield', I contacted Roy Lewis of the Keepsake Press, who produced his hand-set limited editions in a shed at the bottom of his London garden. As well as 'Woods beyond a cornfield' he published a small collection of my concrete (or shape) poems.

At Huddersfield Polytechnic there was the time and encouragement to pursue new ideas in one's subject. Part of the English Department's work was with students in the Education Department who were training to teach and it was in looking for new approaches to poetry that they could make in schools that I investigated the possibilities of concrete (or shape) poetry, to see how children liked it. (They enjoyed a kind of poetry their parents had never heard of.) I have given an account of this in my *Seeing your meaning* which was published by the Polytechnic. In retirement I still go into schools and conduct workshops in concrete poetry.

Birthplace	Austerfield, south Yorkshire
Brothers/sisters	One brother
Schools	Austerfield Primary, Doncaster Grammar
Further education	Christ Church College, Oxford University
Favourite sport	Athletics
Musical interest	Classical music
Favourite drink	Tea, with one sugar
Best TV programme	'Tour de France'
Best radio programme	'Composer of the week'
Best holiday	A week in Scarborough (at age 5)
Favourite book (as a child)	*Treasure Island* by R. L. Stevenson
Favourite poets	Robert Frost, Edwin Morgan, Elizabeth Bishop, Charles Causley
Comment on 'green' issues	It should be a warning to us that jungle is now growing in great cities of the past
Hobbies	Walking
Collections	Paintings and drawings by people I know
Ambition	To walk at least once all the footpaths on the Ordnance Survey map sheet 110
Preferred transport	Bicycle

Racing cyclist

His feet clipped to it, he turns the treadmill
Of his double chainwheel, in highest gear.
The early morning mist on the level road
Through the low-lying countryside
Retreats before him, dragging its cloak
Over the hedges, the lines of poplar trees
And towns and villages with cheering crowds,
The sun, like everyone else, coming out to watch.

For miles he himself and the riders beside him
Seem to him to be standing still,
All moving at the same high speed.

Under welcoming banners and past advertisements,
Low on the handlebars, he ducks the air
That blocks his way and clutches at his clothes,
Keeping level above all with himself
And not a second behind the best he can do.

He rides as surely as if his narrow tyres
Fitted into a groove already there
Or followed a chalk line drawn to the finish
Where people leap up at the roadside,
Beckoning and calling a winner out of the pack.

FROM Form photograph

17   His being the best footballer in the form
Is like his having money in later life –
Boys offer him sweets and want to carry his bag;
And his father's playing part-time professionally
Still counts when the goals are only piled-up coats
Like being related to aristocracy.
Lucky for him to have his life's complexities
Stand on the touchline for a time
While growing older means one size bigger ball:
But even in the game where skill can keep him
Out of trouble he doesn't like being hurt.

18   Officially bad, he looks long-suffering and pale
From staying up too late to watch his anti-heroes
On the telly, skipping breakfast next day
To get to school. Rimless spectacles
Of tiredness rim his eyes; his nails are long
And his feet are dirty. Behaviour and misbehaviour
Boring his matter-of-factness alike,
He moves more easily from fault to fault
Than other boys, like screwed-up cellophane
Gliding in the wind along the gutter.

Poppy

Daffodil

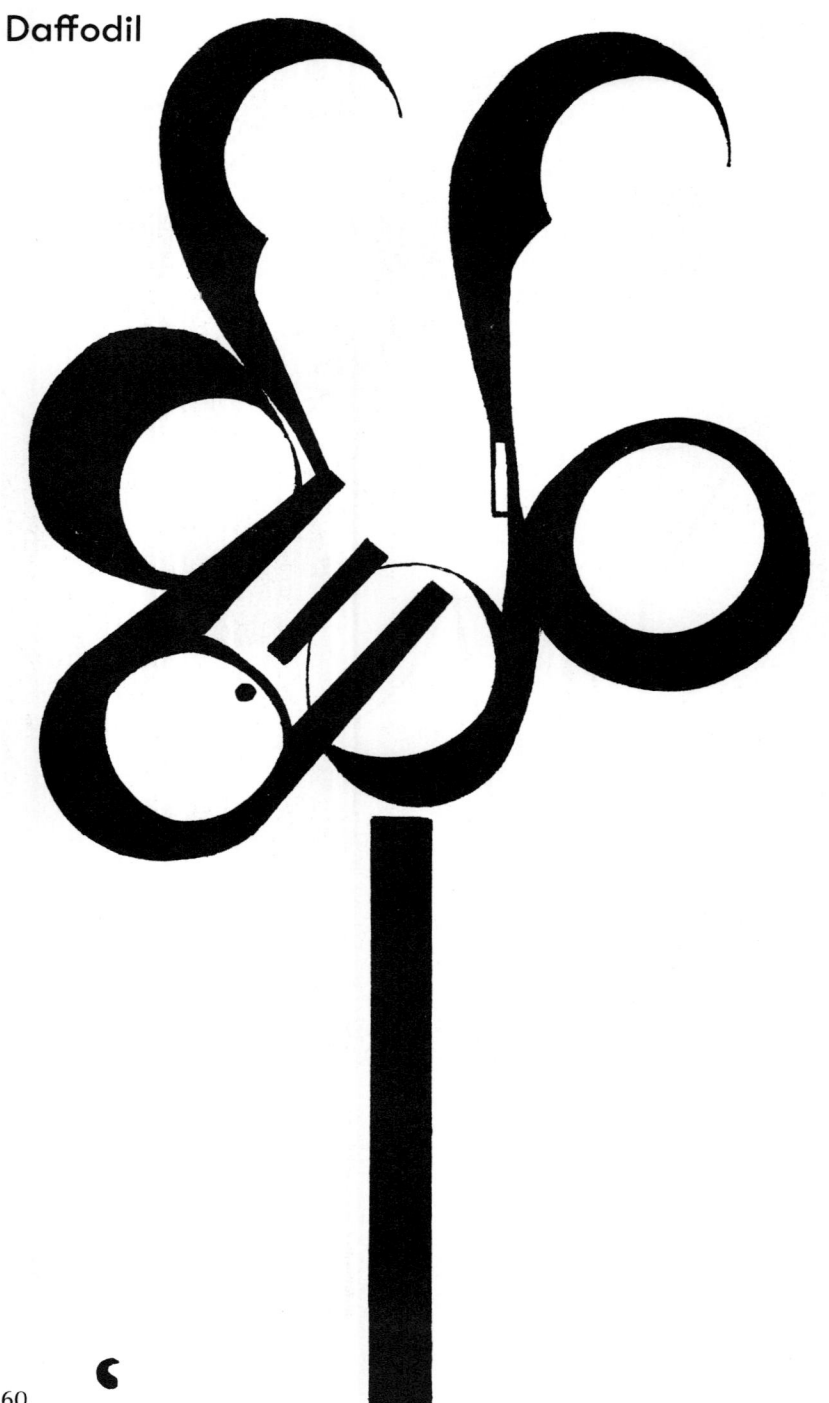

Rose

FROM Woods beyond a cornfield

As I write, the red machines
Descend from the narrow road to the fields,
Monsters with a birdlike brain
At the funnelled end of the chute for the grain.
They roll up lengths of the carpet of corn
And lay behind them the unbaled straw.
No reaper and binder whirling its arms
Like a landborne paddle-steamer,
No sheaves to stook and lead to barns,
No threshing time – all left behind
Like the sickle and the scythe;
No crowds of helpers and spectators –
Only the solitary driver;
No obvious end to the superfield
Where over long stubbles moves a weasel
With the flowing easy line
Of a flourish of copperplate writing.
Where will he and the others who used to use
The hedges to live in be rehoused?
That wildness that runs or runs in the blood
Has nowhere now to go but the wood.

Mick Gowar

Introduction

I began writing poetry – as everyone does – at school. At first, it was simply part of the 'job' of being a pupil along with doing sums, PE, science and writing stories.

But in my teens, writing poetry became more personal; a hobby; something I did without being told to. My poems became a sort of diary, expressing to some extent what I was feeling and thinking, but much more reflecting what I was reading at the time and what I *wished* I was experiencing and feeling but wasn't.

I continued to write intermittently for the next ten years, but I always felt very dissatisfied with what I wrote. Then, when I was 28, I rediscovered children's poetry through helping – in a very menial way – to organise a children's poetry festival. About 10 minutes into the first reading I knew that *this* was the sort of poetry I wanted to write and should write.

I went home, wrote some poems, and showed them to Ruth Craft, the writer who was also the organiser of the festival. She gave me great encouragement, advice, and helped me put together a short manuscript which she sent to her publishers. That was the start of my first book, *Swings and Roundabouts*.

Although most people assume that getting a first book published is the most difficult step for a writer, the greatest challenge is to build a career out of writing. A writer receives ten per cent or less of the cover price of a book in royalties. Consequently, very few writers can actually make a living by simply writing.

Over the last ten years I have gradually put together a career of sorts by combining poetry and fiction writing with part-time editing and giving readings and performances in schools, libraries, colleges and festivals. It's a fairly precarious living and, contrary to popular opinion, being almost constantly hard-up does *not* improve your writing: too often it forces you to rush through the book in order to negotiate a contract for the next book.

Apart from being about childhood or early adulthood, I don't think my poems have any strong common themes or messages. What I do think a lot of my poems have in common is that most of them are fictional and are written as monologues to be

64

'spoken' by a character I've created. This is the style of the
poems 'Pocket money', 'Famous last words' and 'Media studies'.

Occasionally I do write poems based on my own experience;
where the 'I' in the poem is actually me. One such poem is 'The
hawk in the train'. These tend to be poems which are written
much more for the page; for one reader at a time, and not for
public performance.

I tend to write poems in bursts of about six months, and then
not write for a couple of months. Since I began writing seriously
and professionally I have become much more self-critical. I set
myself difficult forms to write in and I tend to write longer and
more complex story-poems, often with more than one 'voice'.

At the moment I am working on a new collection of poems
and a new novel, and at the same time editing a collection of
short stories for one publisher and a series of four
autobiographical books by leading teenage writers for another. I
also have a pretty full diary of readings and performances for the
next six months. I am extraordinarily lucky; I am able to do
what I enjoy most – write – for a living. Although the job does
have its niggles and frustrations, I know that I wouldn't be
happy doing anything else.

Birthplace	Harrow, Middlesex
Brothers/sisters	Two sisters
School	Longfield Primary, Harrow Weald Grammar
Further education	Cambridgeshire College of Arts and Technology, Kingston Polytechnic
Favourite sport	Used to play squash and golf
Musical interest	Play the guitar. Enjoy listening to Lyle Lovett, Randy Newman, Wagner, Vivaldi
Favourite food	Mussels served in a creamy sauce
Favourite drink	Greene King bitter beer, Armagnac
Best TV programme	Woody Allen films, spy thrillers. Never miss 'Whose line is it anyway?'
Best radio programmes	'Today', 'World at One'
Travels abroad	Singapore, Canada
Favourite book (as a child)	*The story of the Amulet* by E. Nesbit
Favourite poets	W.H. Auden, Seamus Heaney, Sylvia Plath, Ted Hughes, Vernon Scannell, Craig Raine, Wendy Cope, Kit Wright, Roger McGough, Brian Patten
Comment on 'green' issues	The destruction of the rainforests, pollution of the seas, and the build-up of greenhouse gases will not be stopped in time to prevent catastrophe
Hobbies	Playing the guitar, reading
Ambition	To collaborate with a musician to create an opera
Pets	Cat called 'Hansel'
Preferred transport	Inter-city train with a proper restaurant car

Pocket money

'I can't explain what happens to my cash,'
I can, but can't – not to my Mum and Dad.
'Give us 10p or get another bash' –

That's where it goes. And though their questions crash
Like blows, and though they're getting mad,
I can't explain what happens to my cash;

How can I tell the truth? I just rehash
Old lies. The others have and I'm the had:
'Give us 10p or get another bash.'

'For dinner, Dad? . . . Just sausages and mash.'
'That shouldn't make you broke by Wednesday, lad.'
I can't explain. What happens to my cash? –

My friends all help themselves. I get the ash
Of fags I buy and give, get none. 'Too bad.
Give us 10p or get another bash.

For being you.' And still I feel the thrash
Of stronger, firmer hands than mine; the sad
Disgust of living like a piece of trash.
I can't explain what happens to my cash.
'Give us 10p or get another bash.'

Alsoran

Your chest hurts twice as bad,
your legs weigh twice as much
when you're alone, adrift
and twenty yards behind the pack.

That special pain that creeps
from chest to shoulder, stabs
beneath the collar bone
and drains all energy away.

Why keep going why keep
thumping on through thick and
thin can't think can't
hardly breathe can't

catch them up can't
keep it up can't
give up now can't face the end
can't win can't stop can't

With easy flowing strides the Blond God
laps you saps
each last despairing flailing
ounce of energy each

Smooth as a tank he glides –
Head Boy next year,
a Scholarship the next and
here, this afternoon, the 1500 metres.

He stands beside the finish being sporting –
the tape sliced,
clean as a whistle,
his from the starting gun:

he's hardly damp. You're sweating like a pig,
wheezing like a broken mattress;
you stagger to a stop,
fall on your knees and puke your dinner up.

With sympathetic smile, he
nimbly skips aside;
you labour on,
his running shoes unsoiled.

Media Studies

She is my homework for tonight.
My Media Studies project's nearly done,
I've nearly filled my folder, but a bit
From 'Panorama' always gets you extra marks.

I switched on at the part the trailer showed –
A girl like me, but younger, 'in the club'.
She fidgets in the posh chrome/leather chair –
So small her feet don't reach the floor.

She says: 'I want someone to love me, only me
More than anyone else in all the world.'
Her boyfriend's far too young to marry, and besides
She doesn't really like him any more.

The baby's all she wants, and that's enough.
She knows for sure the kind of life they'll share –
She won't be like a Mum, they'll grow up mates
And both go down the Disco Saturday night.

She knows, just knows it's going to be a girl.
She'll call her Carly, dress her up real nice
Look after her and that, all on her own,
She talks as if a baby's just a doll!

It's later, trying to write it up – I can't explain . . .
But somehow, what I mean is that it's wrong
To show it all on telly, wrong to pry –
What did she know? She's just a kid, that's all.

How can I put it in my folder, get it marked?
It's someone's life, how can you grade that B or C?
Is that all that her interview was for –
A pass or fail in someone else's CSE . . . ?

Oh yeah?

Every day I come in good as gold,
I've got them fooled – they can't catch me!
Yes, I'll listen – but I won't be told.
Every day I come in good as gold,
Register ... then disappear. I'm free!
Every day I come in good as gold,
I've got them fooled – they can't catch me!

Famous last words

'I won't be late back. I'm going to Jon's party –
it's only down the road . . .'

Why won't you *listen?*
Just let me explain –
Please? Give me a chance,
It won't happen again.
    Look, it wasn't my fault.
    No, it wasn't my fault:
        It was all 'cos the bus didn't come.

The 99 bus –
Oh, didn't I say?
The bus from the disco
(It was miles away!)
    Well, the bus didn't come,
    And that's why, Mum,
        I didn't get home until quarter to one
            When I said I'd be just down the road.

Jon's party? Oh, that
Was a right load of tat . . .
    Well, actually it was OK,
        But Dave didn't know anybody and so
        He got all shirty and wanted to go.
Then Joe says: 'I know a party – not far.
Let's ring up my Dad and we'll go in his car!'

So we went to this other place,
I don't know where,
But the food was all gone
And the parents were there!
    Then Dave says: 'It's poxy!
    Let's all share a taxi
        And go to this disco I know.'

72

So we had a good laugh
In the taxi till half
   The way there we were all cracking up
   At this really good joke,
   When the cab-driver bloke –
For no reason at all –
Goes right up the wall
   And says: 'Right! You can get out and walk!'

So we finally get there:
It's 'Jackets and Ties
Over-21s only'.
We give it a try.
   And we're told to 'get lost!'
   What a cheek!
     So we go to the bus-stop,
     We wait at the bus-stop –
       And the bus doesn't come.

So, that's why, Mum,
I didn't get home until quarter to one
When I said I'd be just down the road.

... Oh, no! That's not fair!
You don't understand:
   I couldn't say no.
   I couldn't not go.
     It *wasn't* my fault,
     No, it wasn't my fault –
       It was all 'cos the bus didn't come ...

The hawk in the train

Springtime in Cambridgeshire. An elderly Paytrain
Limps across the grey-green fens
Under a leaden sky. I sit beside the window
Trying not to look outside. 'Brandon –'

The guard growls. 'Next stop, Brandon.'
The carriages totter over the rusty points.
The ancient diesel engine shudders
To a halt. No one gets out.

Then a sudden twitter of excitement:
Two young men, each with a falcon on his wrist,
Have climbed aboard. Two kids rush up
To pet the birds – are stopped,

Warned to approach slowly, quietly.
'Then maybe – if you're very careful...'
Helmeted like medieval knights, the hawks
Accept the tentative, one-fingered strokes

As tribute. One lifts a foot in slow salute
Exposing cruel talons. The children shrink back,
Giggling nervously, and are called back to their seats
By parents anxious at the sight of claw and beak.

Freed, the two men take the empty seats
In front of me. They nod a friendly greeting,
Hoping for a chat. Not native fen-men, obviously.
The two blind hawks sit motionless.

I ask them if they've been to some Country Fair
Demonstrating Falconry (out here, you see,
We're very keen on killing birds). No, no! They're
Both appalled at the use of hawks for blood sports.

No. These birds are working birds, on contract
To the US Air Force Tactical Bombing Wing.
The runways, so they tell me, in the spring
Are plagued by flights of nesting birds.

(This is the Pentagon's nightmare:
A bird flies into the intake of a jet
Taking off *and armed*, and in a flash –
No more eastern England...)

So these two birds are flown –
Once, twice a week – along the runways.
Airborne deterrence, and it works.
Somewhere behind us, an F1-11

Climbs into the grey sky, heading east.
Hearing the roar, the younger hawk
Jerked from his coma, shrieks:
'A-Wake! A-Wake! A-Wake!'

Song

Here.
To be
warm and quiet,
  alone,
    myself,
      quite separate.

Let them
(below)
crash bang and bellow,
row and bawl –
              I'll

          Stay
          right here
          upstairs

              myself
              alone
              quite separate.

The last ham

This is Papa-Oscar-Echo-Tango...
   Calling Yankee-Oscar-Uncle
This is Papa-Oscar-Echo-Tango...
   Calling Yankee-Oscar-Uncle

This is Papa-Oscar-Echo-Tango...
   Do you read me?
This is Papa-Oscar-Echo-Tango...
   Do you read me?

This is Papa-Oscar-Echo-Tango...
   Does anybody read me?
This is Papa-Oscar-Echo-Tango...
   Does anybody read...?

This is Papa-Oscar-Echo-Tango...
   Is *anybody* there?
This is Papa-Oscar-Echo-Tango...
   Is anybody there *at all*...?

This is Papa-Oscar-Echo-Tango –
   Mayday! ... Mayday! ... Mayday! ...
   Mayday!
   Mayday! ... Mayday! ... Mayday! ...
   Mayday!
   ... ——— ... ——— ... ——— ————————

Wendy Cope

Introduction

One evening in 1980, not long after my first appearance in print, I had a drink with another poet.

'Everyone who becomes a poet,' she said. 'begins writing in childhood.'

'I didn't,' I responded.

'Yes, you did, Wendy,' she insisted. 'You must have done.'

As she spoke, I remembered that she was right. It came back to me: the exercise books I'd filled with stories when I was six or seven, the terrible poems I hid inside my five-year diary when I was fourteen. And the diary itself, of course. That was writing too. I'd been telling people that I didn't start writing until I was 27 and it wasn't true.

We're all obliged to put pen to paper while we're at school. Some of us choose, at an early age, to do it in our spare time as well. In my case the urge to write only broke through intermittently but the urge to read was always very strong. Bookworms don't all grow up to be writers but I think most writers were bookworms when they were small.

Though my parents had both left school when they were fourteen, I was fortunate enough to grow up in a house that had books in it. When I was too little to read to myself, my mother and grandmother read me stories, and my father loved to recite the poems he had learned by heart in his schooldays: 'The Burial of Sir John Moore', Macaulay's 'Horatius' and numerous others. One Christmas, after I'd grown up and left home, I gave him a book called *Parlour Poetry*, which includes some of his favourites. 'It's all right for you,' commented my mother a few weeks later. 'You don't live here. That book has really got him going and I have to listen to it all day long.'

Despite my father's liking for poetry, I much preferred prose. It wasn't until I was an adolescent, studying for O- and A-level English Literature that poems began to get to me. In the fifth form my favourites were Hardy, Yeats and James Elroy Flecker. In the sixth form I fell in love with Keats.

At university I read History, and poetry faded out of my life again until I began working as a primary school teacher, reading poems to children and encouraging them to write their own. After a gap of more than ten years I began writing again in my spare time – writing poems, and reading poems with tremendous curiosity and excitement. This time the interest lasted and it gave a whole new direction to my life. Even if I never got a single word into print, I decided, I wanted to work at writing poems and learn to do it better. A lot of people, it seems to me, never have the good fortune to find out what they really want to do with their lives. I was one of the lucky ones.

Lucky up to a point, anyway. Discovering that you want to be a poet has its drawbacks. Even if you do get published (and this isn't easy), you won't make much money. Some poets have jobs, others get by on the fees from poetry readings, bits of journalism and radio, judging competitions, writing essays for educational books. At present I am in the second category. Most of the time I'm busy meeting deadlines or travelling around the country. But when the day's work is done, I sometimes have time to sit down with a notebook and write the things I want to write, just as I did when I was a child.

Birthplace	Erith, Kent
Brothers/sisters	One sister
School	Farringtons School, Chislehurst
Further education	St Hilda's College, Oxford University
Favourite sport	Swimming
Musical interest	Play piano, guitar, recorder
Favourite food	Wholemeal bread
Favourite drink	Champagne
Best TV programmes	'Capital City', 'LA Law'
Best radio programme	'Any Questions?'
Travels abroad	USA, Canada, Israel, Poland and most countries in Western Europe
Favourite book (as a child)	*The Jungle Book* by Rudyard Kipling
Favourite poets	William Shakespeare, A. E. Housman, Emily Dickinson, Marina Tsvetayeva, Dorothy Parker, Lewis Carroll, Philip Larkin, Keats
Comment on 'green' issues	We're all green nowadays
Hobbies	Singing songs and hymns, taking short walks
Ambition	To be on 'Desert Island Discs'
Preferred transport	Car, feet, ship, train (but not London underground)

Huff

I am in a tremendous huff –
Really, really bad.
It isn't any ordinary huff –
It's one of the best I've had.

I plan to keep it up for a month
Or maybe for a year
And you needn't think you can make me smile
Or talk to you. No fear.

I can do without you and her and them –
Too late to make amends.
I'll think deep thoughts on my own for a while,
Then find some better friends.

And they'll be wise and kind and good
And bright enough to see
That they should behave with proper respect
Towards somebody like me.

I do like being in a huff –
Cold fury is so heady.
I've been like this for half an hour
And it's cheered me up already.

Perhaps I'll give them another chance,
Now I'm feeling stronger
But they'd better watch out – my next big huff
Could last much, much, much longer.

Roger Bear's football poems

Three cheers for Spurs!
They beat Stoke!
Glad I'm a football fan.
Glad I'm a bloke.

––––––––––

Who beat Liverpool
Then beat them again?
Tottenham Hotspur –
A bunch of real men.

––––––––––

Tottenham lost
And I am sad.
Sometimes it's difficult
Being a lad.

––––––––––

Spurs beat Newcastle,
Just like I reckoned.
Spurs are brilliant
And now they are second.

Will they beat Everton?
We'll have to see.
Please get a ticket
For Wendy and me.

Stephen

whose viewing habits had tragic consequences

Shed a tear for Stephen Kelly,
A boy addicted to the telly.
As the hands crept round the clocks,
Stephen sat before the box,
Evenings, mornings, afternoons,
Watching quiz shows, films, cartoons,
'Play School', 'Coronation Street' –
The habit's very hard to treat.

He wouldn't go to bed at night
Without first putting up a fight:
'Oh Mum, it's only half past ten –
Let me see *Dracula* again!'
And very young he'd learned the trick
Of missing school by acting sick,
So he could view from nine till three
Hours and hours of Schools TV.

Dad thought a video recorder
Might help to cure his son's disorder.
'If we can put the shows on tape,'
He said, 'perhaps that square-eyed ape
Will shift himself out of his chair
And get some exercise and air.'
But oh how wrong he was! The boy
Watched twice as much with this new toy –
The good, the middling and the rotten –
The real world was quite forgotten.

One day the TV set broke down;
Mum telephoned a shop in town;
Men came and put it in a van.
'Please mend it quickly as you can,'
Begged Steve. He went to bed and pined
For 'Name that Tune' and 'Mastermind'.
He grew confused and weak and ill –
He couldn't live without 'Grange Hill'.

84

Six days went by and on day seven
Stephen passed away to Heaven,
Asking with his final breath,
'Is there telly after death?'

The orange

At lunchtime I bought a huge orange –
The size of it made us all laugh.
I peeled it and shared it with Robert and Dave –
They got quarters and I had a half.

And that orange, it made me so happy,
As ordinary things often do
Just lately. The shopping. A walk in the park.
This is peace and contentment. It's new.

The rest of the day was quite easy.
I did all the jobs on my list
And enjoyed them and had some time over.
I love you. I'm glad I exist.

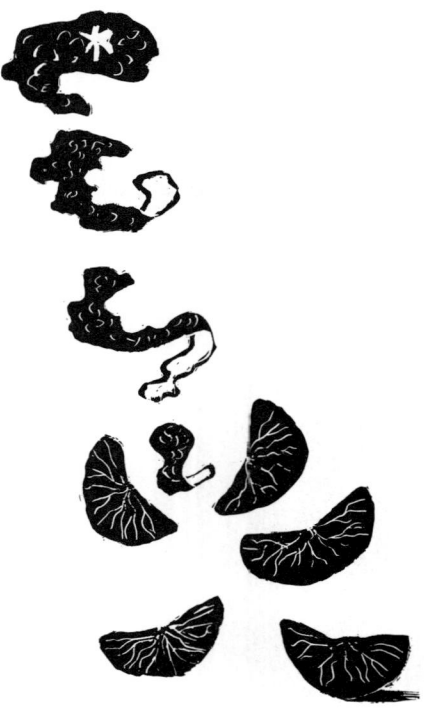

Tich Miller

Tich Miller wore glasses
with elastoplast-pink frames
and had one foot three sizes larger than the other.

When they picked teams for outdoor games
she and I were always the last two
left standing by the wire-mesh fence.

We avoided one another's eyes,
stooping, perhaps, to re-tie a shoelace,
or affecting interest in the flight

of some fortunate bird, and pretended
not to hear the urgent conference:
'Have Tubby!' 'No, no, have Tich!'

Usually they chose me, the lesser dud,
and she lolloped, unselected,
to the back of the other team.

At eleven we went to different schools.
In time I learned to get my own back,
sneering at hockey-players who couldn't spell.

Tich died when she was twelve.

On finding an old photograph

Yalding, 1912. My father
in an apple orchard, sunlight
patching his stylish bags;

three women dressed in soft
white blouses, skirts that brush the grass;
a child with curly hair.

If they were strangers
it would calm me – half-drugged
by the atmosphere – but it does more –

eases a burden
made of all his sadness
and the things I didn't give him.

There he is, happy, and I am unborn.

Advertisement

The lady takes *The Times* and *Vogue*,
Wears Dior dresses, Gucci shoes,
Puts fresh-cut flowers round her room
And lots of carrots in her stews.

A moss-green Volvo, morning walks,
And holidays in Guadeloupe;
Long winter evenings by the fire
With Proust and cream of carrot soup.

Raw carrots on a summer lawn,
Champagne, a Gioconda smile;
Glazed carrots in a silver dish
For Sunday lunch. They call it style.

David Ashbee

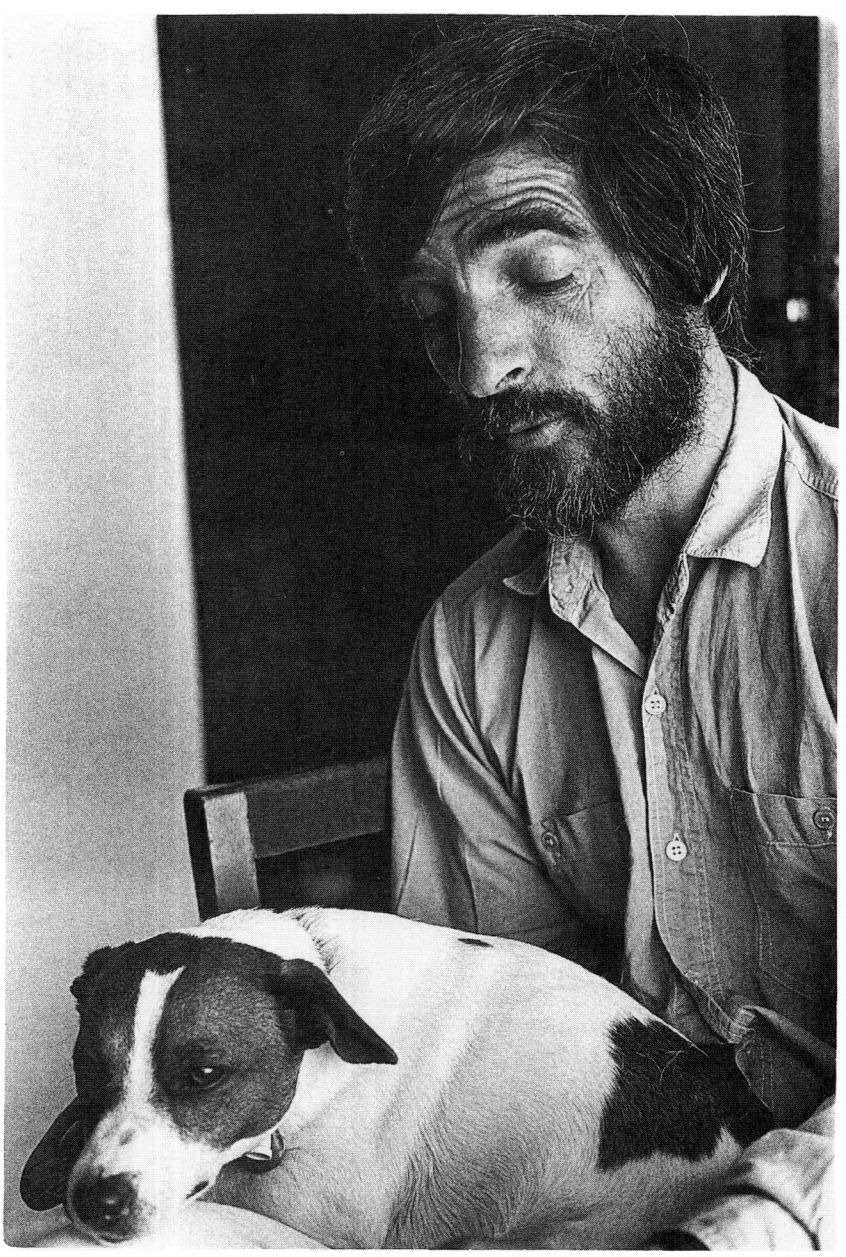

Introduction

I've been an English teacher for twenty years but I've written
poetry for at least thirty. My earliest efforts were published in the
school magazine. Then at college I got a chance to publish an
Arts Festival magazine, and I met other emerging writers. We
decided to read our poems and sing folk songs around other
colleges in London. This was a great experience, and when I
moved back to my native Gloucestershire I took over the running
of a similar group. It was called 'Holub , because the person who
started it was a fan of the Czech poet Miroslav Holub. At about
the same time, a local sculptor made a bronze statuette of a hare
which he wanted to be awarded annually in a local poetry
competition. For years I organised the competition, and through
it and the 'Holub' group I've met hundreds of poets and shared
their work. It's also provided a group to read poems with.
Getting poems published is difficult, but testing poems in public is
vital for me. Sometimes I never realise how good or bad a poem
is, or where it needs changing, until it's read aloud.

The chance to get my first book published came out of the
blue. Stephen Stuart-Smith was taking over a successful poetry
press called 'Enitharmon' and was looking for unpublished poets.
Someone told him about me. He liked my work, and I was again
lucky to meet someone who believes in the power of live
readings.

Another poet and teacher published at the same time, Nick
Stimson, said that he writes to find out who he is. I realised that
was true for me. I am most myself when teaching English to a
good class, reading my poetry to a live audience, or struggling to
compose a poem. I also enjoy country walks, yoga, badminton,
watching Gloucester play rugby, and being with my two teenage
children. But it would all seem a bit pcintless without the poetry,
the readings, and exploring it with others.

One thing I am keen on is getting poems into a form. At
school we encourage pupils to write free verse, without rhyme or
jog-trot rhythm, because they haven't learned to focus on the
best words to put across their feelings. But this has given poetry
a poor image, and makes some people write poetry that is only
prose chopped into random lines. Some present-day poets seem to
lack a sense of form or rhythm. Some actually believe that so

long as you say what you want, the organisation happens automatically. I don't think it often does. Someone once said, 'poetry is 10 per cent inspiration, 90 per cent perspiration', and that's what I believe. Poets who complete a poem quickly (I can when I'm lucky) are drawing on a lot of experience. But there's benefit in leaving that poem to settle for a week or so. As a home wine-maker, I call it 'throwing a sediment'.

One of the exercises I enjoy is working an idea into a particular form. 'Nettles and ivy' is an example of that. In my notebook, that poem was just a series of different length lines. At a poetry workshop we were shown a poem in which the lines rhymed in a particular pattern and echoed from one verse to another. So I reworked my notebook jottings into that form.

What you say in a poem doesn't have to be important. It can be whimsical, pretty, or just plain daft, but a poem can come from it. When you do manage to communicate something important, buried deep inside you, and get it into a well-worked form and rhythm, then share it with someone who says, 'Hey, that's good!' – well, that's one of the finest experiences you can have.

Birthplace	Cheltenham
School	Sir Thomas Rich's Grammar, Gloucester
Further education	Goldsmiths' College, University of London
Favourite sport	Rugby union (supported the 'Cherry and Whites' – Gloucester Rugby Club – for 35 years)
Musical interest	Play guitar. Like modern jazz, piano, country and western, sixties rock, and Vaughan Williams
Favourite food	Homemade pizza, or Tandoori chicken
Favourite drink	Dry red wine, real ale
Best TV programme	News
Best radio programme	'The Rocker Returns'
Travels abroad	Holidays in Europe
Favourite books (as a child)	*The Beano Annual* (1956), Eric Leyland's *Red Flame* books
Favourite poets	William Shakespeare, Gerard Manley Hopkins, Wallace Stevens, Ivor Gurney
Comment on 'green' issues	I find these issues annoyingly fashionable in a world where there are more important priorities, but a good step away from materialism
Hobbies	Photography, watercolour painting
Ambition	To retire from teaching and own a large house (with fine views) where poets and musicians can meet
Pets	My son's Jack Russell, called Tex
Preferred transport	Motorbike in summer, Volvo car in winter, trains when I'm feeling rich, shanks's pony through woods

Nettles and ivy

after James Stephens

Against the sunwarmed Cotswold wall
April nettles, fierce young bloods,
are practising their scowls.

Practise their scowls for when they're tall,
waver in the wind like blustering woods
as they jostle cheek by jowl.

And jostling cheek by jowl, the ivy leaves,
translucent on their haze of silver tracks,
drink the sun's strength in.

Drink strength in and stretch towards the eaves,
to bear the Cotswold farmhouse on their backs
when clouds edge black and shadows lengthen.

Small objects

('Small objects to represent our times are sometimes
placed in the foundations of a new public building
for future discovery. What items would you choose
for this purpose, and why?'
      Question on English examination paper)

Small objects
to represent our times
– a pocket PacMan,
    Rubik's Cube, ignition key,
    Coke-can ring-pull, birth-pill foil,
    eraser tinted with strawberry essence,
    a blank-faced watch –

are sometimes placed in the foundations
of a new public building
– dole centre, bingo hall,
    skating-rink, urinal,
    missile station, sauna bath,
    hypermarket, jail,
    burger bar, bierkeller, discothèque, boutique,
    sex-shop, sweet-shop, sweat-shop, bus-stop,

– these few examples should suffice –

for future discovery
    by Martian? mutant? monk?
    or our children's children's children?
    gooseberry-hairy or fallout-bleached,
    clawing at the brickwork
    for memento
    or crust –

what items would you choose
for this purpose
and

Why?

95

Hoover

Call me a sucker? By making a nothing
I take all in; a mechanical snout
that gropes under skirtings for secreted filth,
renders to the widow her Lost Coin
with a rattle.

Aye, whiner and windbag. But don't be without me
before Christmas, cocktails, or such celebrations.
My belly is a bag of spent days
bound for the trashcan.
I scour the path of soles.

Dust have you sown, so you shall reap.
At your spickest hours I confront you
with this, your inheritance,
that speckles you constantly
but unheeded.

Roller coaster

It's a long way down
but over quick;
the kite of a scream
is winched back in,
as serpent cables tighten
the rack they undergo.
Cars grind up
a corkscrew track
to a deeper
stomach-churning drop.

And who they are up there
we never know;
to hear their torn recanting
is enough;
they have chosen,
paid and chosen, and now
they pay again,
exposed to our stares.
For who can pass and not
look up, to see them
balanced, ready to drop
with a squeal that pinches nerves?

Clattering trucks disgorge
a tottering cargo,
swallow more:
huddling girls who blush through candyfloss,
swaggering boys, urgent for ordeals.

It's a long, long way up.

Their world tilts, like a painting,
shakes and screams;
while we stand watching,
impotent, remote,
with one foot in their dreams.

The man who waves at cars

He waves at all the cars.
Uncertain whether he knows us or is crazy,
most of us wave back.
It gets to be a habit.

For months I never saw him,
never missed him,
for you don't miss a wave
when your foot is down.

Perhaps, wherever he had been,
he took time to adjust,
to recognise the regulars,
but his gesture came once more –

a stick this time, shaken
with a grim determination
against whatever had laid him low
– damned if he couldn't wave.

From childhood mists, his counterparts
come swimming. Like ruddy Jack,
bulldog-jawed, potato-sack man
who hailed in the same brash way.

Streets full of veterans;
one-legged newsvendor, hawking
headlines from the kerb;
bandaged phantom at graveyard gates;

another who cursed his fat mongrel
then tommy-gunned the buses;
he calls them all back
with his grim wave.

Always car-bound, unable to stop,
when I've seen him,
as if in rushing by
we taunt him with what passes:

as they all will soon,
these men who stalk the streets on sticks,
wearing their wounds and memories
under their coats, like medals.

Night wind

Boot-studs on the felting
splinter our sleep.

Ears clenched with commotion,
nerves padlocked into fear,

the body's deadweight
hunched in a dream-fug.

Light shunts against walls –
the clang of wagons

and smokestack roar
as a coal-train thunders through

the tunnel of our head.
Hill rock stacked above.

Egg

roof: shell
floor: shell
walls: shell
doors: none
windows: none

imagine what it must be like,
struggling, barely alive
in a tangle of fluid
a bit like snot

they say he works hard to escape,
a top-notch safebreaker
with a Black-and-Decker beak
to perforate the walls
of his pre-cast cell

but he's not yet born,
according to the files
he's non-existent

I wonder what work I did,
in the womb's dark cave,
what rocks I heaved aside
just to get here on time.

Yesterday, I took an egg,
(fifty pence for six from Gateway),
held it above the pan's sharp edge,
and cracked it.

Poets' choice of poems from the past

Jenny kiss'd me

Jenny kiss'd me when we met,
  Jumping from the chair she sat in;
Time you thief, who love to get
  Sweets into your life, put that in!
Say I'm weary, say I'm sad,
  Say that health and wealth have miss'd me,
Say I'm growing old, but add,
  Jenny kiss'd me.

Leigh Hunt (1784–1859)

John Cotton comments...

I choose this poem because it is beautifully constructed and written. It captures a moment of special pleasure quite exactly.

It is about a great truth – that nothing lasts for ever, but the poem is gently defiant about it. It is also a fine example of an enjoyable sadness. Is it a specially British thing to find pleasure in melancholy? Surely not!

Winter

When icicles hang by the wall,
  And Dick the shepherd blows his nail,
And Tom bears logs into the hall,
  And milk comes frozen home in pail,
When blood is nipp'd, and ways be foul,
Then nightly sings the staring owl, Tu-who;
Tu-whit, tu-who – a merry note,
While greasy Joan doth keel the pot.

When all aloud the wind doth blow,
  And coughing drowns the parson's saw,
And birds sit brooding in the snow,
  And Marian's nose looks red and raw,
When roasted crabs hiss in the bowl,
Then nightly sings the staring owl, Tu-who;
Tu-whit, tu-who – a merry note,
While greasy Joan doth keel the pot.

William Shakespeare (1564–1616)

Julie O'Callaghan comments . . .

I like this poem because it gives me a special pair of glasses that allow me to see a real village in the 1500s. Dick is suffering from chilblains, Tom is stoking the fire, Joan is greasy from cooking, poor Marian has a cold like those whose coughing drowns out the parson's sermon. It is a Brueghel painting in words.

The knee

A lone knee wanders through the world,
  A knee and nothing more;
It's not a tent, it's not a tree,
  A knee and nothing more.

In battle once there was a man
  Shot foully through and through;
The knee alone remained unhurt
  As saints are said to do.

Since then it's wandered through the world,
  A knee and nothing more.
It's not a tent, it's not a tree,
  A knee and nothing more.

Christian Morgenstern (1871–1914)

Roger McGough comments . . .

When I first read 'The knee' in my late teens it seemed so fresh and surreal, so 'un-English' in fact. Even now, it manages to catch me off guard.

Inversnaid

This darksome burn, horseback brown,
His rollrock highroad roaring down,
In coop and in comb the fleece of his foam
Flutes and low to the lake falls home.

A windpuff-bonnet of fawn-froth
Turns and twindles over the broth
Of a pool so pitchblack, fell-frowning,
It rounds and rounds Despair to drowning.

Degged with dew, dappled with dew
Are the groins of the braes that the brook treads through,
Wiry heathpacks, flitches of fern,
And the beadbonny ash that sits over the burn.

What would the world be, once bereft
Of wet and of wildness? Let them be left,
O let them be left, wildness and wet;
Long live the weeds and the wilderness yet.

Gerard Manley Hopkins (1844–1889)

Stanley Cook comments...

This poem has the right sound, suggesting a stream completing an obstacle course of rocks down the mountainside. It also gives a perfect picture in words: for example, no one is ever going to equal 'the beadbonny ash' as a description of the mountain ash.

The donkey

When fishes flew and forests walked
  And figs grew upon thorn,
Some moment when the moon was blood
  Then surely I was born;

With monstrous head and sickening cry
  And ears like errant wings,
The devil's walking parody
  On all four-footed things.

The tattered outlaw of the earth,
  Of ancient crooked will;
Starve, scourge, deride me: I am dumb,
  I keep my secret still.

Fools! For I also had my hour;
  One far fierce hour and sweet:
There was a shout about my ears,
  And palms before my feet.

       G. K. Chesterton (1874–1936)

Mick Gowar comments...

I first read 'The donkey' when I was 12 or 13. What appealed to
me was, firstly, the idea that every creature – no matter how
ugly, no matter how humble – can have its day of glory; and
secondly, the fierce energy of the language.

Unlike a lot of the stories I read and enjoyed then, I still find
reading 'The donkey' enjoyable and thrilling. Now, I can
appreciate the skill and craft of the writing as much as the ideas
and vividness of the descriptions. It is, I suppose, a definition of
what a really good poem is and how it works: different levels of
enjoyment and stimulation, brought into being through a
'collaboration' between the poem and the reader.

When in disgrace with Fortune and men's eyes

When in disgrace with Fortune and men's eyes,
I all alone beweep my outcast state,
And trouble deaf heaven with my bootless cries,
And look upon myself, and curse my fate,
Wishing me like to one more rich in hope,
Featur'd like him, like him with friends possess'd,
Desiring this man's art, and that man's scope,
With what I most enjoy contented least;
Yet in these thoughts myself almost despising,
Haply I think on thee, and then my state,
Like to the lark at break of day arising
From sullen earth, sings hymns at heaven's gate;
   For thy sweet love rememb'red such wealth brings
   That then I scorn to change my state with kings.

William Shakespeare (1564–1616)

114

Wendy Cope comments...

A couple of years ago I was asked to do a Valentine's Day
reading of some of my favourite love poems. I had to practise
and practise reading this one aloud, until I could get to the end
without dissolving into tears. The final couplet is especially
moving. And it's interesting to know that Shakespeare sometimes
felt depressed and inadequate and envious of other people's
talents – worth remembering when you're feeling low yourself.

Ypres-Minsterworth
(To F. W. H.)

Thick lie in Gloucester orchards now
   Apples the Severn wind
With rough play tore from the tossing
   Branches, and left behind
Leaves strewn on pastures, blown in hedges
   And by the roadway lined.

And I lie leagues on leagues afar
   To think how that wind made
Great shoutings in the wide chimney,
   A noise of cannonade –
Of how the proud elms by the signpost
   The tempest's will obeyed –

To think how in some German prison
   A boy lies with whom
I might have taken joy full-hearted
   Hearing the great boom
Of autumn, watching the fire, talking
   Of books in the half gloom.

O wind of Ypres and Severn,
   Riot there also, and tell
Of comrades safe returned, home-keeping
   Music and autumn smell.
Comfort blow him and friendly greeting,
   Hearten him, wish him well.

Ivor Gurney (1890–1937)

OM THE PAST • POETS' CHOICE OF POEMS FROM THE PAST • POETS' CHOICE OF POEM

David Ashbee comments...

Ivor Gurney is bound to be a source of joy to a poet living and born in Gloucester. This poem is one of his best crafted, and manages to be a poem from the trenches, a personal tribute, and a nature poem all at once. It is all the more poignant when one knows the life histories of the two men, Gurney and his friend F. W. Harvey.

Write your own poems

When reading this book you will have noticed that different poets write very different poems. Some writers (like Roger McGough) use humour, while others (like John Cotton and Irina Ratushinskaya) make great use of the senses and memory. You can attempt to create your own poems, using this section of the book to get started.

Riddles

Riddles are 'give-us-a-clue' poems. John Cotton's 'Totleigh Riddles' (page 14) demonstrate the idea, which is to disguise the poem's subject. The reader's task is to find the answer.

Take an everyday classroom object – door, window, ceiling light, notice board – and look at it long and hard. Note down five or six factual observations, as shown here:

1 It stand on four legs.
2 The top is marked with carvings and ink stains.
3 It is made of a dark wood.
4 There are knots and lines in the wood.
. 5 It stays in this room year after year.

From the notes you must now create a riddle in poem form. The aim is to make the writing interesting for the reader.

Classroom riddle

Like a horse, it stands on four legs
and is the colour of wholemeal bread.
It is scarred
with initials and ink stains,
and bears the burden of books and arms
with just the occasional groan.
See the contour lines,
the maps of islands on its surface.
It stands still,
never moves from one year to the next.

(Answer: a table)

Tankas

The tanka is a long-established poem structure from Japan. It is big brother to the haiku, having two extra lines. Like the haiku it is based on a syllable count.

Line 1	5 syllables
Line 2	7 syllables
Line 3	5 syllables
Line 4	7 syllables
Line 5	7 syllables
Total	31 syllables

Attempt a series of four tanka poems taking the seasons as a theme. Spring, for example, could emerge something like this:

Spring tanka

Snowdrops appear first,
then crocus, then daffodil,
but the rain's icy
and winds swoop down from the North.
Sun is a pale, watery eye
as the first leaves unfurl, stretch.

Clerihews

Humour seems easy to achieve in writing, but often proves difficult to pin down. The limerick is regarded as humorous, although the clerihew can be more pointed and apt. The Rev. E. Clerihew Bentley invented the structure and set out the rules.

1 Four lines.
2 A rhyme scheme: A A B B
3 The first line is a person's name.
4 The other lines can be any length.

A famous clerihew concerns Sir Christopher Wren.

> Sir Christopher Wren
> went to dine with some men.
> He said, 'If anyone calls,
> tell them I'm building St. Pauls!'

Try writing your own clerihew (or clerihews) about a famous person (or persons), for example, Margaret Thatcher, Madonna, Princess Diana, James Bond, Gazza, Roger McGough, M.C. Hammer.

Memory poems

Julie O'Callaghan's poems often look back to her childhood. She recaptures – for the reader – her experiences of years ago. The source of her writing is her memory.

Try writing a memory poem; in fact, dig deep and recall your very first memory. Perhaps you were only two or three years old. Write down all you can remember. Write quickly without stopping ('automatic writing'). Then redraft the material and begin to give it some shape on the page (verses? short lines? long lines? rhyme?).

You need to ask yourself questions:

1 What details can you remember from all those years ago?
2 Where did the event take place? What was the location?
3 Can you recall any colours? Or weather? Or sounds?
4 Were any other people present?

By the time you reach the third draft you should have a polished and well-constructed memory poem to your credit.

List poems

List poems (see John Cotton's 'Listen' poem, page 12) offer the
reader a pleasurable experience. Try your hand at writing a list
of the quiet sounds or small noises Irina Ratushinskaya might
very well have heard in her prison cell. Remember, the cell is
quiet. You must imagine a list of almost insignificant sounds:
creaks, a bird beyond the bars, a distant shout, footsteps,
scratchings, a whistle, a humming in the air, an insect on the
flagstones, your heart thumping. Give your list poem a special
shape on the page.

Prison cell sounds

The quiet swish of night wind.
A cockroach scuttling across the stone floor.
A sudden, single, faraway shout.
(and so on)

Formal insults

In Africa an ancient form of writing is the formal insult. Usually
a person's face is singled out for the insult treatment. The writer
creates a particularly insulting image (or word picture) for each
facial feature: eyes, nose, hair, ears, mouth, chin, forehead,
cheeks. Again, try to give the poem shape and order.

A face insults poem

Your face!
Your nose is like the droop-ccne of Concorde
with hairs growing down like landing wheels
Your nose!

Your face!
Your hair is like a tangle of old shoelaces,
knotted time and time and time gain.
Your hair!

Index of first lines

Acknowledgements

The series editor and publisher would like to thank the following for permission to reproduce poems:

John Cotton 'Listen', 'In the kitchen', 'Only', 'Totleigh riddles', 'The wilderness', 'They hide to watch me' and 'Moorland signals' reproduced by permission of the author.

Julie O'Callaghan 'The beach trail', 'Happy birthday from Bennigans', 'Swan Lake' and 'A sunny day' from *Taking my pen for a walk* by Julie O'Callaghan, reproduced by kind permission of Orchard Books, London. 'Touring company', piece from 'Edible Anecdotes' (number 9), piece from 'Edible Anecdotes' (number 22) and 'Local man tells of native city' reproduced by permission of the author.

Roger McGough 'The man who steals dreams', 'Green piece', 'Laughing, all the way to Bank', 'The end of summer', 'Three rusty nails', 'Estate' and 'Cardiff 6 pm' reproduced by permission of Peters, Fraser & Dunlop and the author.

Irina Ratushinskaya 'The sparrows of Butyrki', 'But we shall remain', 'Steeply the stars are scattered', 'I will live and survive', 'To my unknown friend', 'I sit on the floor' and 'No, I'm not afraid' reprinted by permission of Bloodaxe Books Ltd from *No, I'm Not Afraid* by Irina Ratushinskaya, translated by David McDuff, Bloodaxe Books, 1986. We also thank Bloodaxe Books for allowing us to use a piece from the introduction to *No, I'm Not Afraid*.

Stanley Cook 'Racing cyclist', extracts from 'Form photograph' (17) and (18), 'Poppy', 'Daffodil', 'Rose' and a piece from 'Woods beyond a cornfield' reproduced by permission of the author.

Mick Gowar 'Famous last words', 'The hawk in the train' and 'The last ham' from *Live Album* by Mick Gowar, published by Viking Kestrel, 1990, copyright © Mick Gowar 1990. 'Pocket Money', 'Alsoran', 'Media Studies', 'Oh Yeah?' and 'Song' from *So Far, So Good* by Mick Gowar, reproduced by permission of Harper Collins Publishers Ltd.

Wendy Cope 'Huff', 'Roger Bear's football poems', 'The orange' and 'Stephen' reproduced by permission of the author. 'Tich Miller', 'On finding an old photograph' and 'Advertisement' from *Making Cocoa for Kingsley Amis* by Wendy Cope, reproduced by permission of Faber and Faber Ltd.

David Ashbee 'Nettles and ivy', 'Small objects', 'Hoover', 'Roller coaster', 'The man who waves at cars', 'Night wind' and 'Egg' reproduced by permission of the author.